Plants

Seeds

Patricia Whitehouse

Raintree

www.raintreepublishers.co.uk
Visit our website to find out more information about **Raintree** books.

To order:
 Phone 44 (0) 1865 888112
 Send a fax to 44 (0) 1865 314091
Visit the Raintree Bookshop at **www.raintreepublishers.co.uk** to browse our catalogue and order online.

First published in Great Britain by Raintree,
Halley Court, Jordan Hill, Oxford OX2 8EJ,
part of Harcourt Education.
Raintree is a registered trademark of Harcourt
Education Ltd.

Editorial: Nick Hunter and Diyan Leake
Design: Sue Emerson (HL-US) and Joanna Sapwell
(www.tipani.co.uk)
Picture Research: Amor Montes de Oca (HL-US)
Production: Jonathan Smith

Originated by Dot Gradations
Printed and bound in China by South China
Printing Company

ISBN 1 844 21067 7
07 06 05
10 9 8 7 6 5 4 3 2

British Library Cataloguing in Publication Data
Whitehouse, Patricia
Seeds
575.6'8
A full catalogue record for this book is available
from the British Library.

Acknowledgements
The publishers would like to thank the following
for permission to reproduce photographs: Amor
Montes de Oca p. **5R**; Bruce Coleman Inc. pp. **5L**
(Michael Gadomski), **12** (Danny Camilli), **23** (pine
cones, Michael Gadomski; point, E. R. Degginger;
stone, Danny Camilli); Color Pic, Inc. pp. **1** (E. R.
Degginger), **14** (E. R. Degginger), **16** (E. R.
Degginger), **22** (seeds, E. R. Degginger), **24** (seeds,
E. R. Degginger); Corbis pp. **17** (Frank Lane Picture
Agency), **19** (Lynda Richardson), back cover
(sunflower seeds, Frank Lane Picture Agency); Craig
Mitchelldyer p. **13**; David June pp. **11**, **23** (stone);
Dwight Kuhn pp. **7**, **15L**, **21**, **22** (wings), **23**
(wings), **24** (wings); Rick Wetherbee p. **18**; Rob and
Ann Simpson p. **20**; Visuals Unlimited pp. **4**
(Images International), **6** (Jerome Wexler), **8** (Mary
Cummings), **9** (Tom Edwards), **10** (Wally Eberhart),
15 (hooks, Walt Anderson), **22** (hooks, Walt
Anderson), **23** (fruit, Tome Edwards; hooks, Walt
Anderson; seedling, Jerome Wexler), **24** (hooks,
Walt Anderson), back cover (fruit, Images
International).

Cover photograph of sunflower seeds reproduced
with permission of Corbis (Frank Lane Picture
Agency)

Every effort has been made to contact copyright
holders of any material reproduced in this book.
Any omissions will be rectified in subsequent
printings if notice is given to the publishers.

Some words are shown in bold, **like this.** You can find them in the glossary on page 23.

Contents

What are seeds?

Seeds are part of a plant.

Some seeds are inside **fruits** and vegetables.

pine cones

pine seeds

Some seeds are inside **pine cones**.

The seeds come out when the pine cone opens up.

5

Why do plants have seeds?

Seeds make new plants.

The new plants are called **seedlings**.

The new plants look just like the plant the seeds came from.

Where are the seeds on a plant?

The flowers of a plant make seeds.

The seeds are part of the **fruit** of a plant.

The seeds might be on the fruit.

They might be inside it.

How big are seeds?

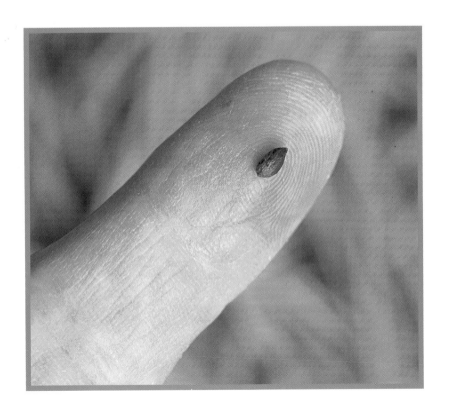

Seeds come in many sizes.

Some seeds are tiny.

Some seeds are very big.

A coconut is a very big seed.

How many seeds can a plant have?

A **fruit** may have just one seed.

An avocado seed is called a **stone**.

Some plants have hundreds of seeds.

Dandelion seeds fly away when you blow on them.

Why do seeds have different shapes?

seed points

The shape of a seed helps it move to a place where it will grow.

Some seeds have points that push into the soil.

seed wings

seed hooks

Wings help some seeds blow in the wind.

Hooks help other seeds hold on to things.

15

What colours are seeds?

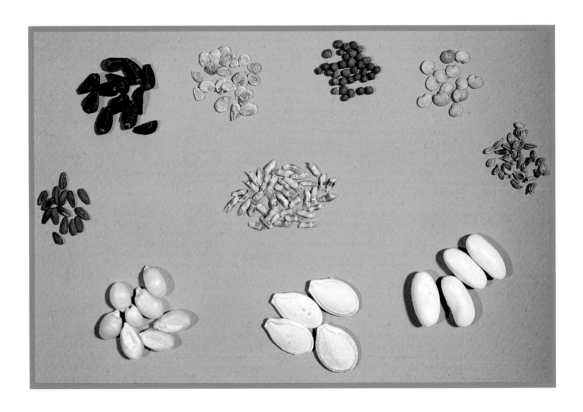

Seeds can be black, brown or yellow.

They can be other colours, too.

Some seeds have patterns on them.

These sunflower seeds have stripes.

How do people use seeds?

People use seeds for food.

We eat some seeds just the way they are.

We crush, squeeze or pop some seeds before we eat them.

We can put seeds in the ground to grow new plants.

How do animals use seeds?

Animals use seeds for food, too.

Birds, squirrels, elephants and monkeys eat seeds.

Some animals eat the seeds right away.

Others save their seeds to eat later.

Quiz

Can you remember what
these seeds do?

Look for the answers on page 24.

?

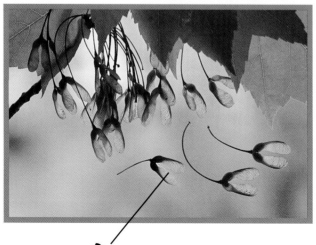

?

?

Glossary

fruit
part of a plant where the
seeds are

hook
curved part that catches
on to things

pine cone
fruit of the pine tree

point
sharp end

seedling
new plant that has just come out
of the ground

stone
the name for a seed if there is only
one in a fruit

wing
part that helps seeds move
through the air

Index

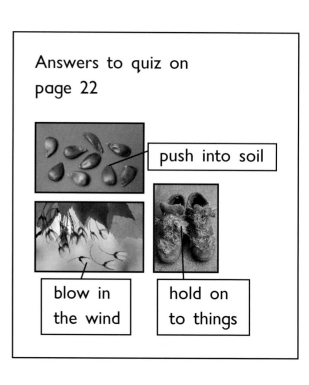

Answers to quiz on page 22

push into soil

blow in the wind

hold on to things

Titles in the Plants series include:

Hardback   1 844 21064 2

Hardback   1 844 21065 0

Hardback   1 844 21066 9

Hardback   1 844 21067 7

Hardback   1 844 21068 5

Hardback   1 844 21069 3

Find out about the other titles in this series on our website www.raintreepublishers.co.uk